HOUGHTON MIFFLIN
HISTORY-SOCIAL SCIENCE
· WORLD HISTORY ·
ANCIENT CIVILIZATIONS

Workbook

. . . .

Visit *Education Place*®
www.eduplace.com/kids

HOUGHTON MIFFLIN   BOSTON

Printed in the U.S.A.

ISBN: 0-618-54058-X

3 4 5 6 7 8 9 10-VHO-14 13 12 11 10 09 08 07 06

HOUGHTON MIFFLIN   BOSTON

Workbook

Contents   page

UNIT 4 ANCIENT ASIAN AND AMERICAN CIVILIZATIONS

Chapter 7 Ancient India

Chapter 8 Ancient China

Chapter 9 Ancient America

UNIT 5 THE ROOTS OF WESTERN IDEAS

Chapter 10 The Hebrew Kingdoms

Chapter 11 Ancient Greece

Chapter 12 Classical Greece

UNIT 6 THE WORLD OF ANCIENT ROME

Chapter 13 The Rise of Rome

Chapter 14 The Birth of Christianity

Chapter 15 Rome's Decline and Legacy

CHAPTER 1 | LESSON 1 The World's Geography

Reading Skill and Strategy

Reading Skill: Summarizing

When you summarize a passage, you identify only its main ideas and important details. Use the questions below to help you identify and record the main idea and supporting details in the section "Looking at Earth." After you have filled in the diagram, identify the main ideas and supporting details of the other two sections in the lesson. Record these in your notebook.

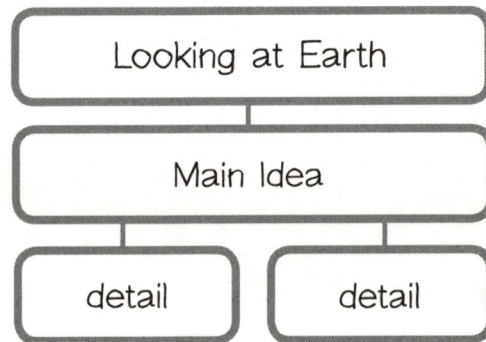

```
┌─────────────────────────────┐
│      Looking at Earth        │
└─────────────────────────────┘
              │
┌─────────────────────────────┐
│         Main Idea            │
└─────────────────────────────┘
        │             │
┌──────────────┐ ┌──────────────┐
│    detail    │ │    detail    │
└──────────────┘ └──────────────┘
```

READING STRATEGY: QUESTIONS

1. Read "Looking at Earth" on pages 9–10. Which of the following best states the section's main idea? Place a check beside the statement and record it in the diagram above.

    _____ Plate movements form mountains and volcanoes and cause earthquakes.

    _____ Earth is made up of continents, landforms, and bodies of water.

    _____ Geographers study Earth and its people.

2. Which of the following statements supports the section's main idea? Place a check beside the two supporting statements and record them in the diagram above.

    _____ Earth is divided into seven continents.

    _____ Two continents—Australia and Antarctica—are islands.

    _____ Earth has many kinds of landforms, but water covers about three-fourths of the planet's surface.

CHAPTER 1 | LESSON 2 How Maps Help Us Study History

Reading Skill and Strategy

Reading Skill: Comparing and Contrasting

This skill helps you discover how two subjects are similar and how they are different. As you read the lesson, record the different characteristics of maps and globes in the "Maps only" and "Globes only" ovals of the Venn diagram below. Write down their similar characteristics in the "Both" oval. Then compare and contrast two types of maps and two periods of mapmaking.

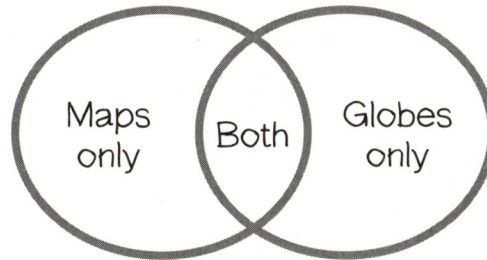

Maps only | Both | Globes only

READING STRATEGY: QUESTIONS

Answer the following questions before you read the lesson.

1. Which of the following words and phrases tell you that two subjects' similarities are being discussed? Which tell you that their differences are being discussed? Write "similarities" or "differences" next to each word or phrase below.

   _____ unlike

   _____ also

   _____ in the same way

   _____ on the other hand

2. Answering which of the following two questions will help you discover some of the differences between a map and a globe? Place checkmarks beside the two questions.

   _____ What characteristics do maps and globes have in common?

   _____ What does a globe show you that a map does not?

   _____ What are the advantages of using a map instead of a globe?

   _____ What do both maps and globes represent?

CHAPTER 1 | LESSON 3 How Archaeologists Study the Past

Reading Skill and Strategy

Reading Skill: Finding Main Ideas

This skill helps you identify the most important point of a passage and the details that support it. After you read the section called "Finding Clues to the Past," record the most important point of the section in the "Main idea" box. Then write down at least two details that support this point. You will also find the main ideas and supporting details of the other two sections of the lesson. Keep in mind that a main idea often comes at the beginning or end of a paragraph.

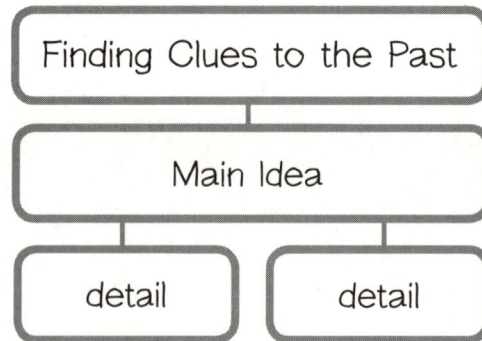

```
┌─────────────────────────────────────┐
│     Finding Clues to the Past        │
└─────────────────────────────────────┘
                  │
┌─────────────────────────────────────┐
│            Main Idea                 │
└─────────────────────────────────────┘
        │                   │
┌───────────────┐   ┌───────────────┐
│    detail     │   │    detail     │
└───────────────┘   └───────────────┘
```

READING STRATEGY: QUESTIONS

Do the following before you read the lesson. Read the paragraphs below. Circle the main idea of each paragraph.

Archaeologists dig up evidence that helps them find out about people who lived long ago. This evidence can include bones and objects that the people made themselves. These objects provide clues about when and how the people lived.

The objects also raise many new questions. Archaeologists often work with other scientists to help them answer these questions. Some scientists help by calculating the age of the bones. Others help archaeologists understand the people's culture, or way of life.

By working together, archaeologists and other scientists can figure out how early people used tools. They can also draw conclusions about when early people developed language and farming. This information has helped the scientists understand how humans have developed over time.

CHAPTER 1 | LESSON 4 How Historians Study the Past

Reading Skill and Strategy

Reading Skill: Categorizing

Categorizing helps you organize similar kinds of information into groups. As you read the lesson, record what you learn about the three main jobs of a historian in the diagram below. List the kinds of questions historians ask in the "Asking questions" box. Jot down the kinds of tools they use in the "Using tools" box. And explain how historians examine evidence in the "Examining evidence" box.

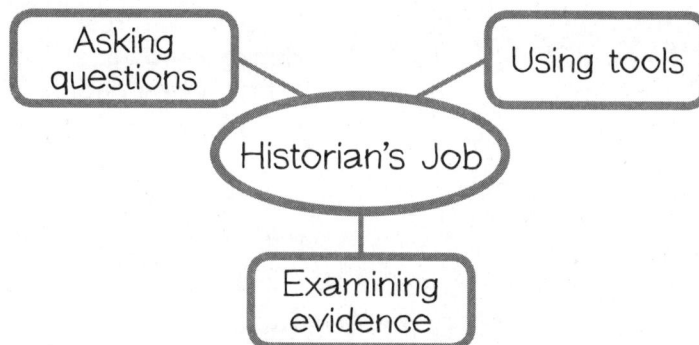

READING STRATEGY: QUESTIONS

Answer the following questions before you read the lesson.

1. Which of the following kinds of information should be grouped under the category "natural disasters"? Place a check beside the three items that belong in the category.

   _____ earthquakes

   _____ wars

   _____ hurricanes

   _____ tornadoes

   _____ car accidents

2. Draw a line connecting the information on the left with the category it should be organized under on the right.

   tools, pottery, weapons   rulers

   language, religion, jobs   artifacts

   letters, diaries, newspaper articles   written sources

   kings, queens, presidents   culture

Reading Skill and Strategy

CHAPTER 1

Reading Skill: Categorizing

As you have learned, categorizing helps you organize similar kinds of information into groups. The information in the visual summary on the right is placed in three categories: geography, culture, and science and technology.

READING STRATEGY: QUESTIONS

A. Use the visual summary to answer the following questions.

1. Under which category do you find information about the methods used to calculate the age of ancient bones?

_____

2. Under which category do you find information about Earth's surface?

_____

3. Under which category do you find information about the progress of early humans?

_____

B. Suppose you wanted to add the following information to the visual summary. Under which category would you place each statement?

1. _____ Geographers use five themes to help them describe Earth.

2. _____ Scientists believe that *Homo erectus* gradually developed into *Homo sapiens*.

3. _____ Cave paintings can tell historians how some early people lived.

The Tools of History

Geography
- Earth is shaped by continents, landforms, and bodies of water.
- Physical features, climate, and vegetation affect where people live.
- People use political, physical, and thematic maps to learn about the world.

Culture
- Primary and secondary sources and oral histories answer questions about the past.
- Our earliest human ancestors first lived in Africa.
- Tools, use of fire, language, and farming developed during the Stone Age.

Science & Technology
- Fossils and artifacts reveal much about human development.
- Dating methods help determine a fossil's age.

CHAPTER 2 | LESSON 1 Hunters and Gatherers

Reading Skill and Strategy

Reading Skill: Summarizing

Summarizing means condensing what you read into fewer words. You state only the
main ideas and the most important details. In your own words, condense the lesson
into two main statements: one about how early humans obtained food and another
about what they did when food was scarce.

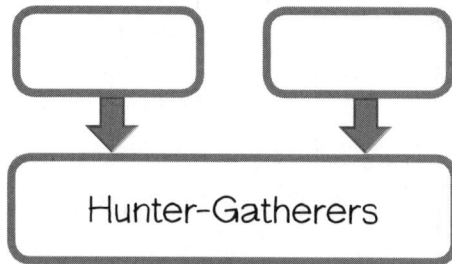

```
┌─────────────────┐        ┌─────────────────┐
│                 │        │                 │
└─────────────────┘        └─────────────────┘
         │                          │
         ▼                          ▼
   ┌──────────────────────────────────────┐
   │          Hunter-Gatherers             │
   └──────────────────────────────────────┘
```

READING STRATEGY: QUESTIONS

1. How did hunters and gatherers obtain their food?

_____

_____

_____

2. What did hunters and gatherers do when food became scarce?

_____

_____

_____

CHAPTER 2 | LESSON 2 Learning to Farm and Raise Animals

Reading Skill and Strategy

Reading Skill: Understanding Cause and Effect

Causes are the events, conditions, and other reasons that lead to an event. Causes happen before the event in time and explain why it happened. Effects are the results or consequences of the event.

As you look over the following lesson, think about the kinds of tools the farmers developed. Also think about what effect these tools had on their efficiency and what effect tools had on their need to move.

Cause	Effects
Agricultural revolution causes changes in tools for growing and harvesting grain.	1.
	2.
	3.

READING STRATEGY: QUESTIONS

1. What effect did new tools have on the efficiency of farmers?

   _____

   _____

   _____

2. What effect did improved efficiency have on the mobility of farmers? Did they have to move around as much?

   _____

   _____

   _____

3. What is the overall name for the shift from food gathering to food raising that produced changes in tools for growing and harvesting grain?

   _____

   _____

   _____

CHAPTER 2 | LESSON 3 The First Communities

Reading Skill and Strategy

Reading Skill: Categorizing

Categorizing means organizing similar kinds of information into groups. Historians categorize information to help them identify and understand historical patterns.

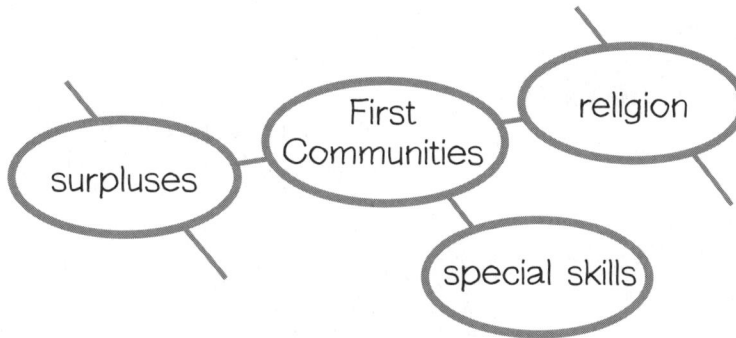

CHAPTER 2

READING STRATEGY: QUESTIONS

1. What sorts of surpluses might villages have been able to accumulate?

   _____

   _____

   _____

2. What sorts of people might have evolved into the first priests?

   _____

   _____

   _____

3. What are some examples of special skills that people in villages developed?

   _____

   _____

   _____

CHAPTER 2 | REVIEW The Earliest Human Societies

Reading Skill and Strategy

Reading Skill: Summarizing

Summarizing means condensing what you read into fewer words. You state only the main ideas and the most important details. In your own words, summarize what you have learned about geography, science and technology, and culture by answering the following questions.

READING STRATEGY: QUESTIONS

1. How did early humans adapt to their environment?

   _____

   _____

   _____

   _____

2. What are some examples of the use of science and technology by early humans?

   _____

   _____

   _____

   _____

3. What are three examples of human culture?

   _____

   _____

   _____

   _____

The Earliest Human Societies

Geography
- Early humans adapted to their environment.
- Hunter-gatherers lived a nomadic life in pursuit of animals.
- Farming developed in many parts of the world.

Science & Technology
- Humans desire to explore the world and solve problems.
- Weapons and tools helped hunter-gatherers to survive.
- New technologies developed to support the agricultural revolution.

Culture
- Early humans developed language, religion, and art.
- Agriculture caused a change in how people lived.
- Simple farming villages developed into complex villages.

CHAPTER 2

CHAPTER 3 | LESSON 1 Geography of Mesopotamia

Reading Skill and Strategy

Reading Skill: Summarizing

The skill of summarizing helps you to record information in a brief way. You will use this skill when you do research for reports and when you take notes to study for tests. Remember that summaries are shorter than the original passage. In the box below, summarize the three sections of this lesson by writing a sentence about each one that restates the most important idea. The sentences are begun for you.

> ### Geography of Mesopotamia
>
> The rivers of Mesopotamia were important because . . .
>
> Mesopotamians watered their crops by . . .
>
> Because of a lack of resources, . . .

READING STRATEGY: QUESTIONS

1. Reread the section, "Fertile Soil." Then on the lines below, write a sentence or two summarizing the main idea of that paragraph.

   _____

   _____

   _____

2. Reread the section, "Mud Houses and Walls." Then on the lines below, write a sentence or two summarizing the main idea of that section.

   _____

   _____

   _____

CHAPTER 3

CHAPTER 3 │ LESSON 2 The First Civilization

Reading Skill and Strategy

Reading Skill: Making Generalizations

A generalization is a broad judgment, or statement, that you make based on specific pieces of information. This skill is useful for seeing patterns in history. On the chart below, record specific examples of each of the five traits of civilization.

Civilization in Sumer	
Advanced cities	
Specialized workers	
Complex institutions	
Record keeping	
Advanced technology	

READING STRATEGY: QUESTIONS

1. Why must a society develop city life before it develops complex institutions? Write your answer as a generalization.

_____

_____

_____

2. How does the invention of advanced technology help create a need for specialized workers? Write your answer as a generalization.

_____

_____

_____

CHAPTER 3

CHAPTER 3 | LESSON 3 Life in Sumer

Reading Skill and Strategy

Reading Skill: Categorizing

When you categorize, you sort information into useful groups. This skill will help you to organize study material and to prepare outlines for papers. Categorize the information about life in Sumer, found in Lesson 3, by recording it on the chart below.

Life in Sumer		
Society	Technology	Writing

READING STRATEGY: QUESTIONS

1. Read the following list of words and phrases. Next to each one, write the number of the category it is most related to: 1. Society 2. Technology 3. Writing

   _____ stylus

   _____ potter's wheel

   _____ plow

   _____ kings and priests

   _____ pictograph

   _____ bronze

   _____ cuneiform

   _____ slaves

2. Sometimes information relates to more than one category. Think about the term *scribe*. Which two categories could you put this in? Explain.

   _____

   _____

   _____

CHAPTER 3

Reading Skill and Strategy

Reading Skill: Making Inferences

The skill of making inferences helps you to understand the importance of what you read. To make an inference, use your own knowledge to come up with ideas about the text.

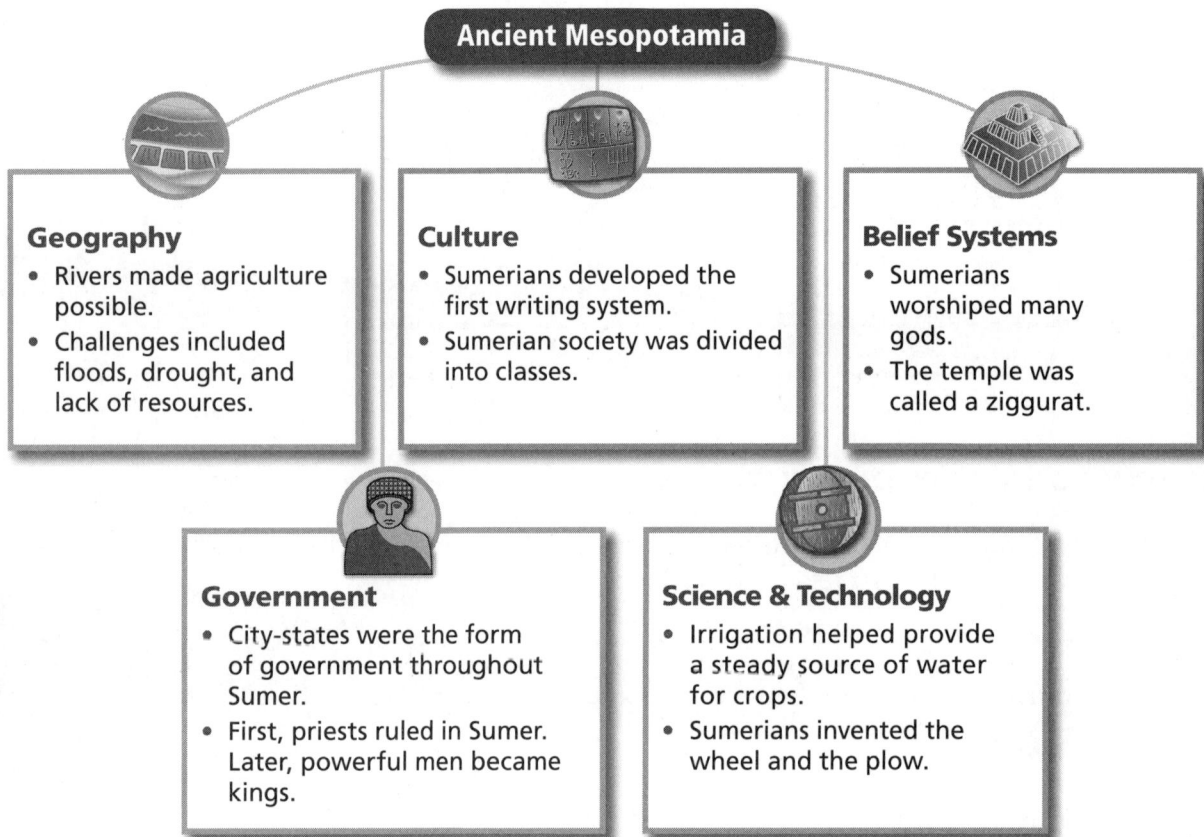

Ancient Mesopotamia

Geography
- Rivers made agriculture possible.
- Challenges included floods, drought, and lack of resources.

Culture
- Sumerians developed the first writing system.
- Sumerian society was divided into classes.

Belief Systems
- Sumerians worshiped many gods.
- The temple was called a ziggurat.

Government
- City-states were the form of government throughout Sumer.
- First, priests ruled in Sumer. Later, powerful men became kings.

Science & Technology
- Irrigation helped provide a steady source of water for crops.
- Sumerians invented the wheel and the plow.

Study the chart below and then answer the questions beneath it by making inferences.

READING STRATEGY: QUESTIONS

1. Review the information in the Science & Technology box. What do you think was one of the main economic activities of Sumer? Why?

   _____

   _____

2. Judging from the information on this chart, what qualities do you think characterized the people of Sumer?

   _____

   _____

CHAPTER 4 | LESSON 1 Mesopotamian Empires

Reading Skill and Strategy

Reading Skill: Summarizing

When you summarize you restate the main idea in your own words. You may to include some important details supporting the main idea. Use the headings to help you look for the main ideas. In the box below write a summary sentence about each of the three topics shown.

Topic	Statement
Geography	
A strong king	
A law code	

READING STRATEGY: QUESTIONS

1. Read the section "The Akkadian Empire." Then check the summary statement you think best summarizes the section.

   ___ Sargon built the Akkadian Empire which was the first empire in world history.

   ___ The Fertile Crescent had many empires including the Akkadian Empire.

   ___ The Akkadian Empire brought together many different people and lands.

2. Read the section "Hammurabi's Law Code." Then check the summary statement you think best summarizes the section.

   ___ Hammurabi wrote a set of laws covering business and property rights.

   ___ Hammurabi's law code was set up to provide justice for many different people in the empire.

   ___ Hammurabi's code was displayed on a pillar so all people could see and read it.

CHAPTER 4

CHAPTER 4 : LESSON 2 Assyria Rules the Fertile Crescent

Reading Skill and Strategy

Reading Skill: Understanding Cause and Effect

A cause may be a person, an event, or an idea that makes something happen. An effect is something that results from a cause. There are many examples of cause and effect in the study of history. The chart below can be used to study the causes and effects of large empires on the lands they control. at the   In the Effect box, write the results of the three causes listed.

Causes	Effects
Assyrian military machine	
Cruelty to captured peoples	
Huge empires	

READING STRATEGY: QUESTIONS

1. Read "A Mighty Military Machine." Then check the statement that you think best describes the cause of fear felt by people who faced the Assyrian armies.

   ____ The Assyrian armies were well-trained, and used cruel tactics to conquer other countries.

   ____ The conquered people believed that the gods helped the Assyrian armies.

   ____The Assyrian armies brought diseases that the conquered people had not been exposed to.

2. Read "Chaldeans Take Assyrian Lands." Then check the statement that you think best describes an effect of the Chaldean takeover of Assyrian lands.

   ____ The Egyptians took over the lands of Syria.

   ____ The Hebrews were taken captive and moved to Babylon.

   ____ The people in the captured lands were grateful for the change.

CHAPTER 4

CHAPTER 4 | LESSON 3 Persia Controls Southwest Asia

Reading Skill and Strategy

Reading Skill: Identifying Issues and Problems

This skill will help you find and understand difficulties faced by a person or a group of people at a certain time. By studying the issues and problems you may better understand the actions of a particular group of people. In the Venn diagram below list the problems faced by Cyrus and Darius as they ruled the Persian Empire.

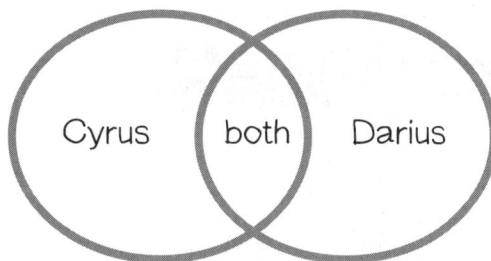

Cyrus   both   Darius

READING STRATEGY: QUESTIONS

1. Read "A Wise Emperor." Then check the question that you might ask about issues or problems while reading this section.

   ___ Why was Cyrus such a good emperor?

   ___ Why did the Hebrews like Cyrus?

   ___ Why was the policy of toleration a good one?

2. Read "Uniting the Empire." Then check the question that you might ask about issues or problems while reading this section.

   ___ Why was uniting the empire important?

   ___ How was the messenger service on the Royal Road set up?

   ___ What are minted coins?

CHAPTER 4

Reading Skill and Strategy

Reading Skill: Categorizing

When you categorize you sort information into groups called categories. Studying categories can help you see information in a different way and recognize patterns that may exist. In the Visual Summary below the accomplishments of the early empires are categorized. What are the categories shown? Why might these categories be important?

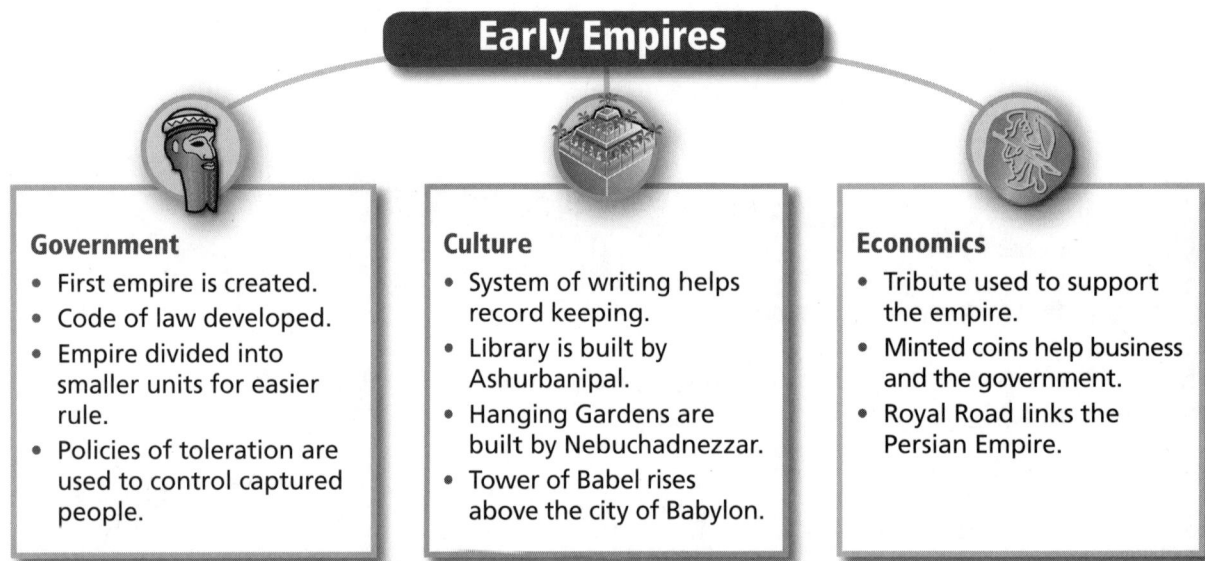

Early Empires

Government
- First empire is created.
- Code of law developed.
- Empire divided into smaller units for easier rule.
- Policies of toleration are used to control captured people.

Culture
- System of writing helps record keeping.
- Library is built by Ashurbanipal.
- Hanging Gardens are built by Nebuchadnezzar.
- Tower of Babel rises above the city of Babylon.

Economics
- Tribute used to support the empire.
- Minted coins help business and the government.
- Royal Road links the Persian Empire.

READING STRATEGY: QUESTIONS

1. Study the Visual Summary. Mark the statement that best shows the relationship between some categorized items.

   ___ Empires needed record-keeping and tribute to run efficiently.

   ___ The Royal Road was a way to get information to Assurbanipul's library.

   ___ Culture and economics really don't have much to do with government.

2. Study the Visual Summary. Mark the statement that best shows the relationship between some categorized items.

   ___ The Royal Road linked Babylon to the Hanging Gardens.

   ___ Tribute and minted coins were helpful to running a government.

   ___ An empire needed some culture to improve the lives of its people.

CHAPTER 4

CHAPTER 5 : LESSON 1 The Gift of the Nile

Reading Skill and Strategy

Reading Skill: Understanding Cause and Effect

A cause is an event. An effect is the result or consequence of the event. One event often has more than one result. Historians examine cause-and-effect relationships to understand how events are related and why they took place. Use the following questions to help you identify the effects of the causes listed in the diagram below.

Causes	Effects
Floods	
New agricultural techniques	
Many land resources	

READING STRATEGY: QUESTIONS

1. Read "Geography of Ancient Egypt" on pages 147–148. Which of the following is an effect of the floods that occurred every year in the Nile River? Place a check beside the statement and record it in the diagram above.

   _____ Heavy rains in Ethiopia caused the Nile to flood every summer.

   _____ The Nile River flooded at the same time every year.

   _____ The floods deposited rich soil along the Nile's shore that was good for growing crops.

2. Read "Land of Plenty" on pages 148–149. What happened as a result of the new agricultural techniques that the ancient Egyptians developed? Place a check beside two results and record them in the diagram above.

   _____ Egyptian farmers expanded their farmland.

   _____ Farmers grew a large variety of foods.

   _____ Egyptians built houses using bricks made of mud from the Nile.

3. Read "Geography Shapes Egyptian Life" on pages 150–151. What happened as a result of the many land resources in Egypt? Place a check beside two results and record them in the diagram above.

   _____ Egypt's economy depended on farming.

   _____ Egyptians mined minerals and precious stones.

   _____ Egyptians fished, hunted, and traded on the Nile.

CHAPTER 5

Reading Skill and Strategy

Reading Skill: Categorizing

Categorizing helps you organize similar kinds of information into groups. As you read the lesson, record what you learn about Egyptian culture in the diagram below. List details about religion in Egypt in the "Religion" box. Write details about jobs and family life in the "Work and family" box. And jot down details about advances in learning in the "Learning" box.

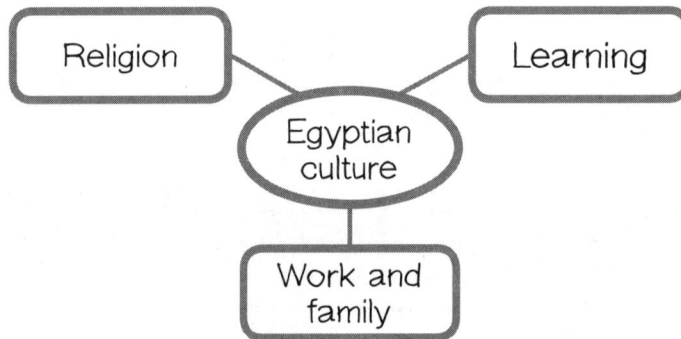

```
  ┌──────────┐                    ┌──────────┐
  │ Religion │                    │ Learning │
  └──────────┘                    └──────────┘
          \           ╭─────────╮        /
           \──────────│ Egyptian│───────/
                      │ culture │
                      ╰─────────╯
                           │
                    ┌──────────┐
                    │ Work and │
                    │  family  │
                    └──────────┘
```

READING STRATEGY: QUESTIONS

Answer the following questions before you read the lesson.

1. Which of the following sections provides details that can be categorized under the heading "Work and family"? Place a checkmark beside the correct section.

    _____ Life for Women

    _____ Geometry

    _____ Life After Death

2. Which of the following sections provides details that can be categorized under the heading "Religion"? Place a checkmark beside the correct section.

    _____ Specialized Jobs

    _____ Astronomy

    _____ Many Gods

3. Under which category would you place each of the following? Write "Religion," "Work and family," or "Learning" beside each statement.

    _____ Egyptians embalmed dead people because they believed they would need their bodies in the afterlife.

    _____ Egyptians took on jobs such as that of a scribe and artisan.

    _____ Egyptians developed the world's first practical calendar.

    _____ The main job of most women was to care for their children and home.

CHAPTER 5 | LESSON 3 The Pyramid Builders

Reading Skill and Strategy

Reading Skill: Summarizing

When you summarize a passage, you identify only its main ideas and important
details. In the diagram below, list the main ideas and important supporting details
about pyramids. You can add as many boxes as you need. Use the subheadings in
"Khufu's Great Pyramid" on pages 166–169 to help you identify main ideas about
pyramids. You can then use these main ideas and details to write a brief summary
about pyramids.

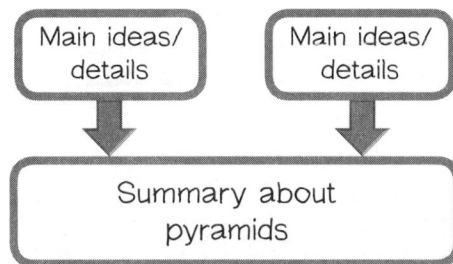

```
┌──────────────┐   ┌──────────────┐
│ Main ideas/  │   │ Main ideas/  │
│   details    │   │   details    │
└──────┬───────┘   └──────┬───────┘
       │                  │
       ▼                  ▼
  ┌──────────────────────────────┐
  │      Summary about           │
  │        pyramids              │
  └──────────────────────────────┘
```

READING STRATEGY: QUESTIONS

Answer the following questions before you read the lesson.

1. Which of the following statements best expresses the main idea under the
    subheading "The Great Pyramid"? Place a check beside the statement and record
    it in the diagram above.

    _____ Khufu's Great Pyramid was the largest pyramid ever built.

    _____ Building the Great Pyramid was hard work.

    _____ A city called Giza was built for the pyramid workers.

2. Which of the following statements best expresses the main idea under the
    subheading "Grave Robbers"? Place a check beside the statement and record it
    in the diagram above.

    _____ Because of grave robbers, pharaohs began building more secret tombs.

    _____ Grave robbers stole treasure and mummies.

    _____ The burial chambers were hidden in mountains near the Nile.

3. Which of the following statements best expresses the main idea under the
    subheading "Inside the Tombs"? Place a check beside the statement and record it
    in the diagram above.

    _____ Wall paintings showed pharaohs enjoying activities.

    _____ Passageways were designed to confuse robbers.

    _____ Tombs were supposed to be the palaces of pharaohs in the afterlife.

CHAPTER 5 | LESSON 4 The New Kingdom

Reading Skill and Strategy

Reading Skill: Explaining Chronological Order and Sequence

Placing events in sequence means putting them in order based on the time they
happened. Understanding the order in which things happened helps you get an
accurate sense of the relationships among events. As you read the lesson, put events
that happened in the reigns of the New Kingdom pharaohs in order. Remember
that dates in the B.C. era should follow in descending order; that is, from greater to
smaller numbers.

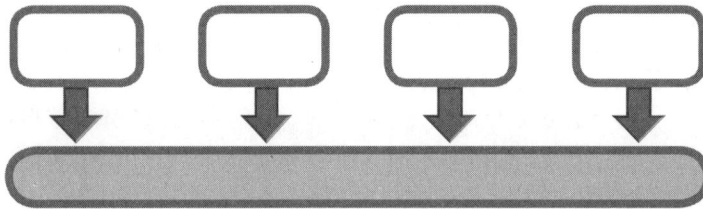

READING STRATEGY: QUESTIONS

Answer the following questions before you read the lesson.

1. What is the correct order of the following dates? Number the dates from 1 to 4.

    _____ 1070 B.C.

    _____ 1353 B.C.

    _____ 1279 B.C.

    _____ 1472 B.C.

2. What is the correct order of the following events? Number the events from 1 to 4.

    _____ Akhenaton becomes pharaoh.

    _____ Hatshepsut declares herself pharaoh.

    _____ Ramses II becomes pharaoh.

    _____ Tutankhamen becomes pharaoh.

CHAPTER 5 | REVIEW Ancient Egypt

Reading Skill and Strategy

Reading Skill: Categorizing

As you have learned, categorizing helps you organize similar kinds of information into groups. The information in the visual summary below is placed in five categories: geography, economy, belief systems, science and technology, and government.

Ancient Egypt

Geography
- Nile provided silt and water, transportation.
- Desert acted as a natural barrier.

Economy
- Traded with parts of Africa, Arabia, and Mediterranean countries
- A prosperous land with many specialized jobs

Belief Systems
- Many gods; pharaoh was one
- Believed in a happy afterlife

Science & Technology
- Developed calendar, astronomy, medicine
- Developed written language—hieroglyphs

Government
- Upper and Lower Egypt united as one country
- Pharaohs and dynasties kept control; priests served as officials

READING STRATEGY: QUESTIONS

Use the visual summary to answer the following questions.

1. Under which category do you find information about Egyptian trade and prosperity?

_____

2. Under which category do you find information about the development of the calendar and written language?

_____

3. Under which category do you find information about the pharaohs and dynasties?

_____

CHAPTER 5

CHAPTER 6 | LESSON 1 Nubia and the Land of Kush

Reading Skill and Strategy

Reading Skill: Explaining Sequence

Sequencing events means putting things in the order in which they happened. Historians need to figure out the order in which things happened to get an accurate sense of the relationships among events. As you read this lesson, figure out the sequence, or time order, of important events.

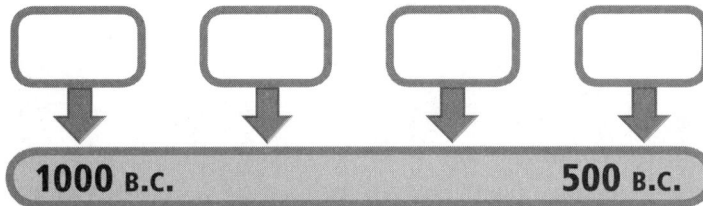

1000 B.C.   **500 B.C.**

READING STRATEGY: QUESTIONS

- Kush becomes a power.

- Egypt rules parts of Nubia.

- Meroë becomes capital of Kush.

- Kush conquers Egypt.

1. Which of the above events happened first?

_____

2. Which of the above events happened last?

_____

CHAPTER 6 | LESSON 2 The Kingdom of Aksum

Reading Skill and Strategy

Reading Skill: Finding Main Ideas

The main idea is a statement that sums up the most important point of a paragraph, a pssage, an article, or a lesson. Determining the main idea will increase your understanding as you read about historic events, people, and places. Main ideas are supported by details and examples. In Lesson 2, look at the main heads in the lesson: The Rise of Aksum, King Ezana Expands Aksum, and Aksum's Achievements. Try to pick out a couple of main ideas under each head.

```
┌──────────┐                              ┌──────────┐
│          │          ╭─────────╮         │          │
└──────────┘          │  The Kingdom      └──────────┘
  1. _____           │  of Aksum│          1. _____
  2. _____          ╰─────────╯          2. _____

        ┌──────────┐
        │          │
        └──────────┘
          1. _____
          2. _____
```

READING STRATEGY: QUESTIONS

1. Why was Aksum's location good for trade?

_____

_____

2. What was King Ezana's effect on Aksum?

_____

_____

3. What were three areas in which Aksum achieved important things?.

_____

_____

CHAPTER 6 : LESSON 3 West, Central, and Southern Africa

Reading Skill and Strategy

Reading Skill: Explaining Geographic Patterns

Identifying and explaining geographic patterns means seeing the overall shape, organization, or trend of geographic characteristics. Seasonal weather cycles are one example of a geographic pattern. Migration routes are another example, as you will see in the section labeled "The Bantu Migrations."

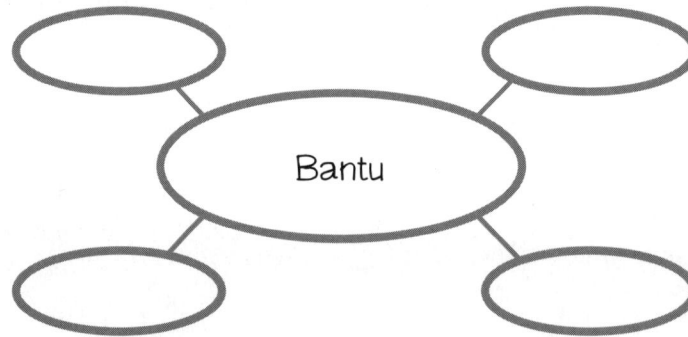

READING STRATEGY: QUESTIONS

1. What are some of the cultural elements that the Bantu took with them on their migrations?

   _____

   _____

2. In what main directions did the Bantu move?

   _____

   _____

CHAPTER 6 | REVIEW Kush and Other African Kingdoms

Reading Skill and Strategy

Reading Skill: Finding Main Ideas

The main idea is a statement that sums up the most important point of a paragraph, a passage, an article, or a lesson. Determining the main idea will increase your understanding as you read about historic events, people, and places. Main ideas are supported by details and examples.

Kush and Other African Kingdoms

Geography
- Nubia and Egypt interacted over the centuries.
- The people of Africa lived in different environments.
- Bantu speakers traveled from West Africa to central and southern Africa.

Government
- The Kush kingdoms conquered Egypt and ruled Egypt and Nubia.
- The kingdom of Aksum absorbed Kush in the region of Nubia.

Economics
- The Kushite kingdom of Meroë was an economic center linking Egypt and the interior of Africa.
- The Nok people were accomplished ironworkers.

Culture
- The kingdom of Aksum converted to Christianity.
- Aksum's achievements in architecture, language, and farming were long-lasting.

READING STRATEGY: QUESTIONS

1. What main geographical feature helped to define the culures of Nubia and Egypt?

_____

2. What form of government ruled in Egypt, Kush, and Aksum?

_____

3. What economic activity permitted Kush and Aksum to prosper?

_____

4. What was the religion of Aksum?

_____

CHAPTER 6

CHAPTER 7 | LESSON 1 Geography and Indian Life

Reading Skill and Strategy

Reading Skill: Making Generalizations

A generalization is a broad judgment that you make about specific pieces of information. This skill is useful for seeing patterns in history. On the chart below, record specific information about the geography of India and its effect on the development of civilization there.

Geography and Indian Life	
Physical geography of India	
Cities in the Indus Valley	
Harappan culture	

READING STRATEGY: QUESTIONS

1. Why did many ancient civilization arise in river valleys such as the Indus River valley? Word your answer as a generalization.

   _____

   _____

   _____

2. Why do large cities need to be governed by strong leaders? Word your answer as a generalization.

   _____

   _____

   _____

CHAPTER 7 | LESSON 2 The Origins of Hinduism

Reading Skill and Strategy

Reading Skill: Summarizing

The skill of summarizing helps you to record information in a brief way. You will use this skill to take notes for studying or while doing research. Remember that summaries are shorter than the original passage. In the box below, summarize the three sections of this lesson by completing a sentence about each one that restates the most important idea. The sentences are begun for you.

```
┌─────────────────────────────────────────┐
│        The Origins of Hinduism           │
├─────────────────────────────────────────┤
│   The Aryans migrated . . .              │
├─────────────────────────────────────────┤
│   Aryan culture changed India by . . .   │
├─────────────────────────────────────────┤
│   The main characteristics of           │
│   Hinduism are . . .                     │
└─────────────────────────────────────────┘
```

READING STRATEGY: QUESTIONS

1. Reread the section "Aryan Beliefs and Brahmanism." Then write a sentence or two summarizing the main idea of that section on the lines below.

   _____

   _____

   _____

2. Reread the section "Many Lives." Then write a sentence or two summarizing the main idea of that section on the lines below.

   _____

   _____

   _____

CHAPTER 7

CHAPTER 7 | LESSON 3 Buddhism and India's Golden Age

Reading Skill and Strategy

Reading Skill: Comparing and Contrasting

You can use this skill to find the ways that things are similar and different. You might apply it to people, cultures, governments, artistic styles, or events. In this way, you will start to see patterns in history. Use the Venn diagram below to compare and contrast two great empires of India.

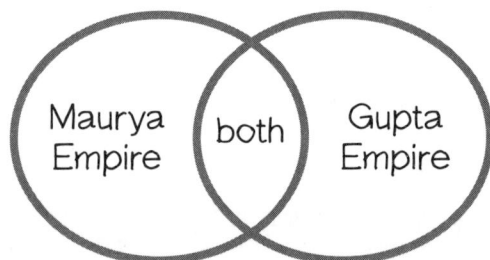

Maurya Empire — both — Gupta Empire

READING STRATEGY: QUESTIONS

1. How did the Maurya and Gupta rulers increase their territory? Compare and contrast their methods.

   _____

   _____

   _____

2. How were Asoka and Chandra Gupta II similar and different?

   _____

   _____

   _____

CHAPTER 7

CHAPTER 7 | LESSON 4 The Legacy of India

Reading Skill and Strategy

Reading Skill: Categorizing

When you categorize, you sort information into useful groups. This skill will help you to organize study material and to prepare outlines for papers. Categorize the information about the legacy of India, found in Lesson 4, by recording it on the chart below.

Legacy of India		
Religion	Arts	Mathematics

READING STRATEGY: QUESTIONS

1. Read the following list of words and phrases. Next to each one, write the number of the category it is most related to: 1. Religion; 2. Arts; 3. Mathematics.

   _____ architecture

   _____ Hindu-Arabic numerals

   _____ *ahimsa*

   _____ Mohandas Gandhi

   _____ decimal system

   _____ zero

2. Reread the section "India's Artistic Legacy" and pay close attention to the information about the visual symbols that represent the Buddha's holiness. Which two categories does this information relate to? Explain.

   _____

   _____

   _____

CHAPTER 7

Reading Skill and Strategy

Reading Skill: Understanding Cause and Effect

An effect is an event or action that is the result of a cause. Historians study effects to understand the long-term impact of events and actions. Learning this skill will help you to see how events across time are connected. Study the visual summary on the right, looking for effects.

READING STRATEGY: QUESTIONS

1. How did belief systems affect Indian government? Explain.

   _____

   _____

   _____

   _____

   _____

2. What aspect of Indian culture affected other Asian societies?

   _____

   _____

   _____

   _____

   _____

Ancient India

Geography
- An early Indian civilization arose near the Indus and Saraswati rivers.
- Monsoons, or seasonal winds, affect India's climate.

Government
- Chandragupta Maurya ruled harshly. He used spies, his army, and many officials.
- Asoka tried to rule peacefully, influenced by Buddhism.

Belief Systems
- Hinduism is a religion that worships deities in many forms and believes in reincarnation.
- Buddhism teaches people to follow a middle way according to the Eightfold Path.

Culture
- Indian artistic styles spread to other regions of Asia.
- Indians invented the zero, Hindu-Arabic numerals, and the decimal system. They were skilled metal workers.

CHAPTER 7

CHAPTER 8 | LESSON 1 Geography Shapes Life in Ancient China

Reading Skill and Strategy

Reading Skill: Explaining Geographic Patterns

Understanding physical and cultural features of a city, state, region, or country can help explain geographic patterns such as economic activities, location of settlements, movement of people, or spread of ideas. Maps are helpful in finding these patterns. Reading the text can also help you find these patterns. In the diagram below, write in the natural barriers found near China's North Plain.

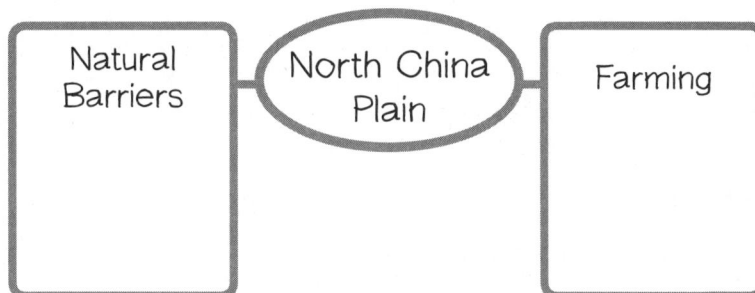

```
┌──────────┐   ╭───────────╮   ┌──────────┐
│ Natural  │───│ North China │───│ Farming  │
│ Barriers │   │   Plain     │   │          │
│          │   ╰───────────╯   │          │
└──────────┘                    └──────────┘
```

READING STRATEGY: QUESTIONS

1. Read the section "Geographic Features of China." Then check the statement that best summarizes a geographic pattern discussed in this section.

    ___ Deserts surround China and isolate it.

    ___ Mountains surround China making most outside contact impossible.

    ___ China has fertile soil in two river valleys.

2. Read the section "Geographic Features of China." Then check the statement that best summarizes a geographic pattern discussed in this section.

    ___ China's physical features are not like those of the United States.

    ___ China had early river valley settlements.

    ___ China's North Plain allows easy contact with the west.

CHAPTER 8

CHAPTER 8 | LESSON 2 China's Ancient Philosophies

Reading Skill and Strategy

Reading Skill: Comparing

The skill of comparing allows you to look at a subject and find similarities and differences among sets of people, places, things, or ideas. First, you should determine the topic of your comparison. Next, look for key words such as *all, both, alike,* or *similarly*. Using these key words will help you find parts of a passage that have similar ideas. In the diagram below, three philosophies are compared. Fill in the chart with similarities or differences in the three philosophies of ancient China.

Legalism	Confucianism	Daoism

READING STRATEGY: QUESTIONS

1. Read the sections "Legalism" and "Confucianism." Then check the question that you might ask to discover differences between the two philosophies.

   ___ Why did people believe there was a need for peace and harmony in China?

   ___ How was the Legalist way of controlling society different from that of Confucianists?

   ___ Which philosophy—Legalism or Confucianism—was more effective in running an empire?

2. Read the section "Confucianism." Then check the statement that best shows a comparison made in that section.

   ___ Confucius believed that all relationships were based on respect.

   ___ Confucius believed that rulers had a responsibility to live correctly.

   ___ Confucius believed it was right to respect older brothers but not younger brothers.

CHAPTER 8 : LESSON 3 The Qin and the Han

Reading Skill and Strategy

Reading Skill: Comparing and Contrasting

Comparing things means looking for similarities. Contrasting things means looking for differences. Looking for similarities and differences between two or more things may help you understand events, ideas, beliefs, or people. Using a Venn diagram is a good way to clearly see the similarities and differences between two things. In the Venn diagram below, compare and contrast the rule of the Qin Dynasty and the Han Dynasty.

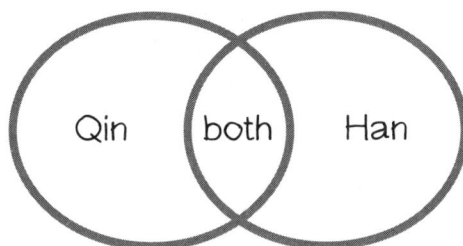

READING STRATEGY: QUESTIONS

1. Read the section "The Han Dynasty." Pick the statement that best shows a contrast between the Qin and the Han dynasties.

   ____ The Qin had a strong central government.

   ____ The Han had lower taxes and less harsh treatment of peasants than the Qin.

   ____The Han followed Confucian ideas.

2. Read the section "Life in Han China." Pick the statement that best shows similarities between Han life and life in the United States.

   ____ Chinese cities were similar to U.S. cities in some ways.

   ____ Chinese ate much more meat and fish than people in the United States.

   ____ Han Chinese farmers used farm equipment that differs from that used by U.S. farmers.

CHAPTER 8

CHAPTER 8 | LESSON 4 The Legacy of Ancient China

Reading Skill and Strategy

Reading Skill: Categorizing

Categorizing means sorting information into groups. Studying the information in a category may help you understand historical events or ideas. After you read a piece of information that includes many details, you should think about what information should be categorized. You should also think about what categories the information might fit into. Then sort the information based on those categories. In the web diagram below, sort information into categories based on the headings in the lesson.

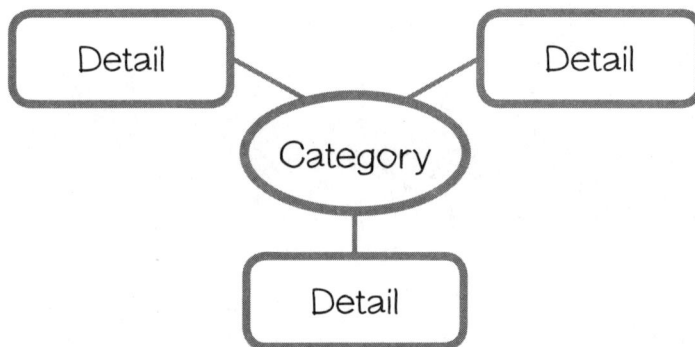

```
  ┌─────────┐                    ┌─────────┐
  │ Detail  │                    │ Detail  │
  └─────────┘                    └─────────┘
        \                          /
         \        ╭────────╮      /
          ────────│Category│──────
                  ╰────────╯
                      │
                 ┌─────────┐
                 │ Detail  │
                 └─────────┘
```

READING STRATEGY: QUESTIONS

1. Read the section "Silk Roads." Then check the set of categories that best shows categories of things that moved on the Silk Roads.

   _____ silk, horses, pottery

   _____ Buddhism, gold, paper

   _____ trade goods, ideas, cultural practices

2. Read the section "Chinese Inventions and Discoveries." Then check the set of items that would be grouped under the category of Chinese inventions and discoveries.

   _____ agricultural tools, paper, silk

   _____ Confucianism, Daoism

   _____ sesame seeds, oil

CHAPTER 8 | REVIEW Ancient China

Reading Skill and Strategy

Reading Skill: Summarizing

When you summarize you restate the main idea in your own words. You also include the important details that support the main idea. Use headings to help you look for the main ideas. Study the visual summary below. Then write a summary sentence about each of the four topics shown.

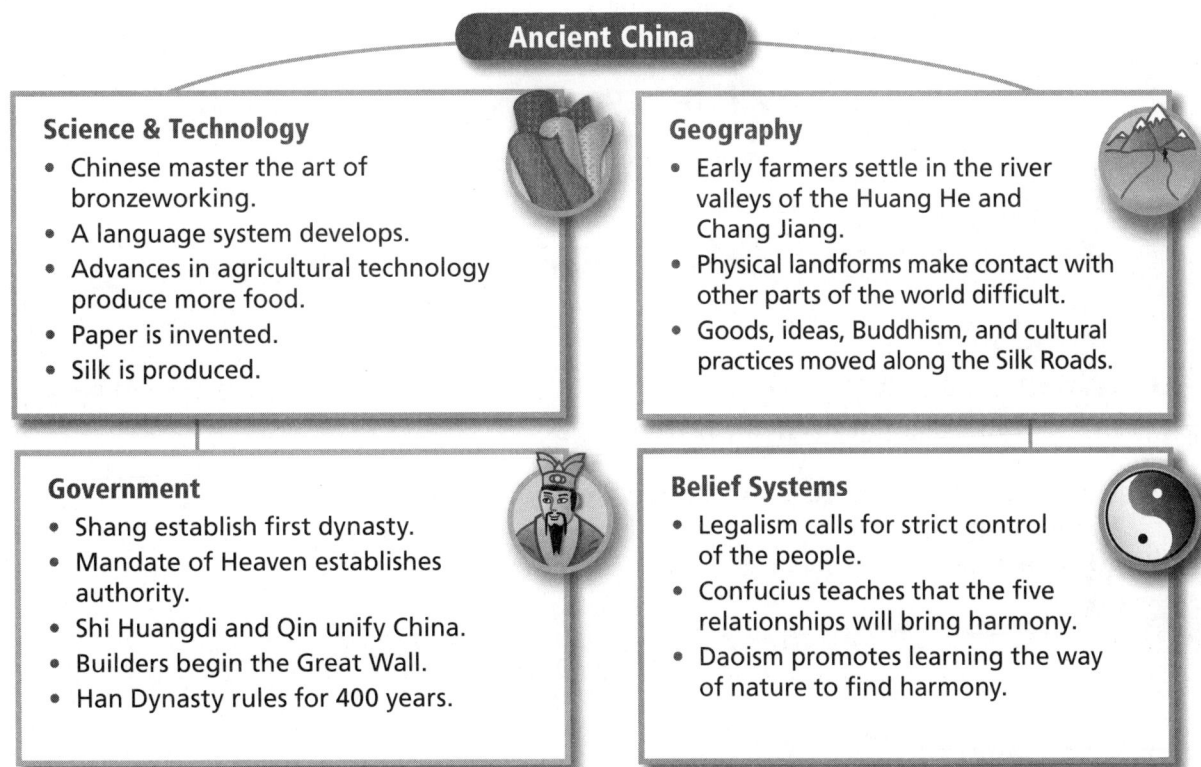

Ancient China

Science & Technology
- Chinese master the art of bronzeworking.
- A language system develops.
- Advances in agricultural technology produce more food.
- Paper is invented.
- Silk is produced.

Geography
- Early farmers settle in the river valleys of the Huang He and Chang Jiang.
- Physical landforms make contact with other parts of the world difficult.
- Goods, ideas, Buddhism, and cultural practices moved along the Silk Roads.

Government
- Shang establish first dynasty.
- Mandate of Heaven establishes authority.
- Shi Huangdi and Qin unify China.
- Builders begin the Great Wall.
- Han Dynasty rules for 400 years.

Belief Systems
- Legalism calls for strict control of the people.
- Confucius teaches that the five relationships will bring harmony.
- Daoism promotes learning the way of nature to find harmony.

READING STRATEGY: QUESTIONS

1. Study the visual summary box labeled "Geography." Then check the statement that best summarizes the information in that box.

____ China's geography isolated it from contact with other river valley civilizations.

____ The geography of China influenced both its settlement and contact with the outside world.

____ China had a river valley civilization like those of the Fertile Crescent and Egypt.

2. Study the visual summary box labeled "Belief Systems." Then check the statement that best summarizes the information in that box.

____ The belief systems of China had three different approaches to ruling the people.

____ The people preferred the use of Daoism as the basic principle in ruling their land.

____ Confucianism was the best way to rule China's huge population.

CHAPTER 9 : LESSON 1 The Geography of the Americas

Reading Skill and Strategy

Reading Skill: Comparing and Contrasting

This skill helps you discover how two subjects are similar and how they are different. As you read the lesson, record the different geographic features of the Andes and Meso-America in the "Andes only" and "Meso-America only" ovals of the Venn diagram below. List their similar features in the "Both" oval.

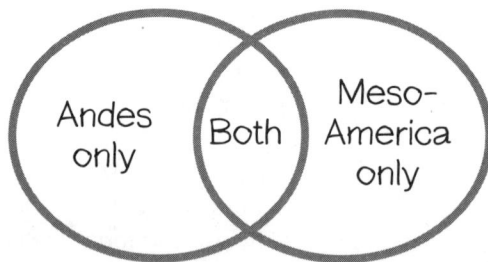

READING STRATEGY: QUESTIONS

Answer the following questions before you read the lesson.

1. Which of the following words and phrases tell you that two subjects' similarities are being discussed? Which tell you that their differences are being discussed? Write "similarities" or "differences" next to each word or phrase below.

   _____ also

   _____ however

   _____ in contrast with

   _____ similarly

2. Answering which of the following two questions will help you discover some of the differences between the geography of the Andes and that of Meso-America? Place checkmarks beside the two questions.

   _____ In what ways are the climates of the Andes and Meso-America similar?

   _____ What natural disasters are both regions subject to?

   _____ How does the environment of the Andes contrast with that of Meso-America?

   _____ How do the physical features of the two regions differ?

CHAPTER 9 | LESSON 2 Ancient Andean Civilizations

Reading Skill and Strategy

Reading Skill: Drawing Conclusions

When you draw conclusions, you analyze what you have read and form opinions about its meaning. To draw conclusions, you look closely at the facts and details presented. In this lesson, you will use the details presented to draw conclusions about three ancient Andean civilizations: the Chavín, the Nazca, and the Moche.

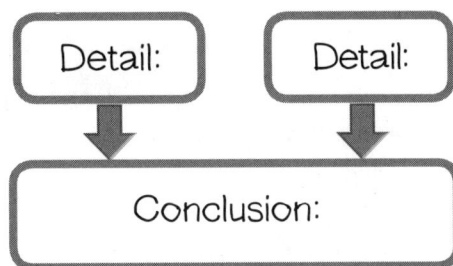

```
  ┌──────────┐     ┌──────────┐
  │ Detail:  │     │ Detail:  │
  └────┬─────┘     └────┬─────┘
       ▼                ▼
  ┌──────────────────────────┐
  │     Conclusion:          │
  └──────────────────────────┘
```

READING STRATEGY: QUESTIONS

1. Read "The Chavín Civilization" on pages 295–296. What conclusion can you draw from the details presented about Chavín religious art? Place a checkmark beside the correct conclusion.

_____ The Chavín were religious and artistic.

_____ The Chavín were not very religious.

_____ Little is known about the artistic style of the Chavín.

2. Read "The Nazca Civilization" on pages 296–297. Which of the following details support the conclusion that the Nazca were highly creative? Place a checkmark beside two correct details.

_____ The Nazca made the Nazca Lines.

_____ The Nazca prospered from around 200 B.C. to A.D. 600.

_____ Little is known about the political and economic structures of the Nazca.

_____ The Nazca civilization is known for its beautiful pottery and textiles.

3. Read "The Moche Civilization" on pages 298–299. Which conclusion about the Moche cannot be drawn from the details in the section? Place a checkmark beside the incorrect conclusion.

_____ Moche nobles exercised a great deal of power.

_____ The Moche learned to survive in their environment.

_____ The Moche believed in and worshiped many gods.

CHAPTER 9 | LESSON 3 The Olmec of Meso-America

Reading Skill and Strategy

Reading Skill: Categorizing

Categorizing helps you organize similar kinds of information into groups. As you read the lesson, record what you learn about Olmec civilization in the diagram below. List details about Olmec cities in the "Cities" box. Write details about Olmec art, religion, and learning in the "Culture" box. And provide details about Olmec influence in the "Legacy" box.

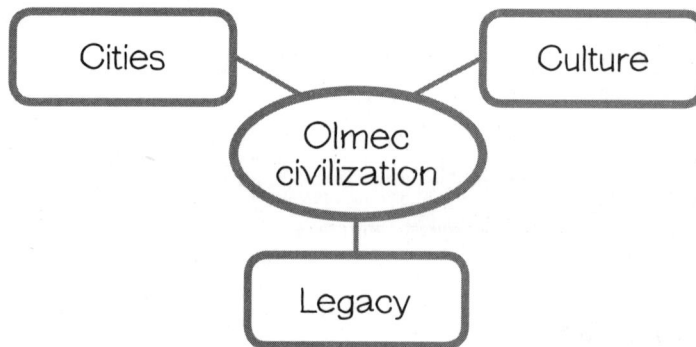

```
   ┌────────┐              ┌─────────┐
   │ Cities │              │ Culture │
   └────────┘              └─────────┘
        \                    /
         \   ╭──────────╮   /
          \  │  Olmec   │  /
             │civilization│
             ╰──────────╯
                  │
             ┌─────────┐
             │ Legacy  │
             └─────────┘
```

READING STRATEGY: QUESTIONS

Answer the following questions after you read the lesson.

1. Which of the following details would you categorize under the heading "Legacy"? Place a checkmark beside the correct detail.

_____ The Olmec left behind their ideas for cities, ceremonial centers, and ritual ball games.

_____ Olmec cities were ruled by powerful dynasties.

_____ Archaeologists found huge stone heads that weigh as much as 20 tons.

2. Which of the following sections provides details that can be categorized under the heading "Culture"? Place a checkmark beside the correct section.

_____ Geography

_____ Olmec Art

_____ Influences

CHAPTER 9 | LESSON 4 The Mayan Civilization

Reading Skill and Strategy

Reading Skill: Summarizing

When you summarize a passage, you identify only its main ideas and important details. Use the questions below to help you identify and record the main idea and supporting details in the section "The Rise of the Maya." After you have filled in the diagram, identify the main ideas and supporting details of the other two sections in the lesson. Record these in your notebook.

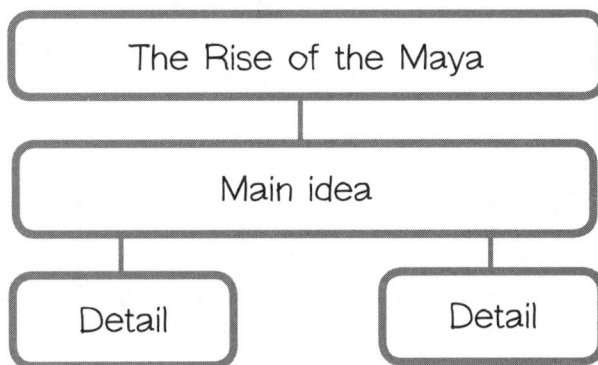

The Rise of the Maya

Main idea

Detail   Detail

READING STRATEGY: QUESTIONS

1. Read "The Rise of the Maya" on pages 307–308. Which of the following best states the section's main idea? Place a check beside the statement and record it in the diagram above.

____ The Mayan civilization, which rose in Meso-America, built magnificient city-states from about A.D. 250 to 900.

____ The Maya began to develop a civilization as the Olmec declined.

____ The period from A.D. 250 to 900 is traditionally known as the Classic Period of Mayan civilization.

2. Which of the following statements supports the section's main idea? Place a check beside the two important details and record them in the diagram above.

____ The city-states were linked through trade.

____ The Maya began to develop a civilization from present-day southern Mexico into northern Central America.

____ During the Classic Period, the Maya built magnificent city-states with temples, pyramids, and plazas.

CHAPTER 9 | REVIEW Ancient Americas

Reading Skill and Strategy

Reading Skill: Comparing and Contrasting

As you have learned, comparing and contrasting helps you discover how two subjects are similar and how they are different. You can use the information in the visual summary on the right to compare and contrast two regions and two civilizations in ancient America.

READING STRATEGY: QUESTIONS

1. According to the information in the "Geography" box, how were the environments of the Andes and Meso-American different? Place a checkmark beside the correct answer.

   _____ Both left behind beautiful artwork.

   _____ Andean civilizations created irrigation systems, while those in Meso-America built great cities.

   _____ The Andean civilizations developed in a harsh environment, while those in Meso-America lived in fertile land.

2. Based on the information in the visual summary, in what way were the ancient American civilizations similar? Place a checkmark beside the correct answer.

   _____ They all developed a calendar.

   _____ They all were talented artists, engineers, and architects.

   _____ They all spread their influence through trade.

Ancient America

Geography
- The Andes provided a harsh environment for the Chavín, Nazca, and Moche civilizations.
- The Olmec and Maya lived in fertile land in Meso-America.

Culture
- Trade helped spread Olmec culture throughout Meso-America.
- Ancient Americans left behind beautiful carvings, pottery, and textiles.
- The Maya built pyramids and temples in their great city-states.

Science and Technology
- The Moche created irrigation systems.
- The Maya developed a calendar and the concept of zero.

CHAPTER 10 | LESSON 1 The Origins of the Hebrews

Reading Skill and Strategy

Reading Skill: Understanding Cause and Effect

Causes are the events, conditions, and other reaons that lead to an event. Causes happen before the event in time; they explain why it happened. Effects are the results or consequences of the event. As you look over the following lesson, think about the effects of Abraham leaving Ur, Moses leading the Hebrews out of Egypt, and Moses climbing Mount Sinai.

Causes	Effects
Abraham leaves Ur.	
Moses leads people out of Egypt.	
Moses climbs Mount Sinai.	

READING STRATEGY: QUESTIONS

1. What was one effect of Abraham leaving Ur?

_____

_____

2. What happened as a result of Moses climbing Mount Sinai?

_____

_____

CHAPTER 10

CHAPTER 10 | LESSON 2 Kingdoms and Captivity

Reading Skill and Strategy

Reading Skill: Explaining Chronological Order and Sequence

Sequencing events means putting things in the chronological order in which they happened. Historians need to figure out the order in which things happened to get an accurate sense of the relationships among events. As you read this lesson, figure out the sequence, or time order, of important events in Hebrew history.

READING STRATEGY: QUESTIONS

- Persians conquer Babylonia.
- Saul becomes king.
- King Solomon dies.
- Assyria conquers Israel.

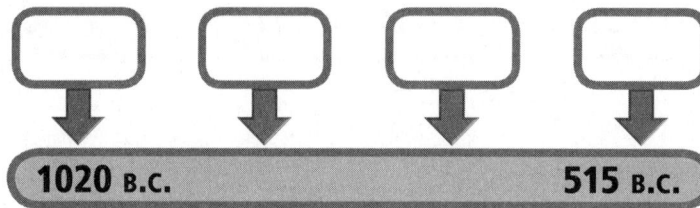

1020 B.C.   515 B.C.

1. Which of the above events happened first?

_____

2. Which of the above events happened last?

_____

CHAPTER 10 | LESSON 3 Rome and Judea

Reading Skill and Strategy

Reading Skill: Comparing and Contrasting

Comparing and contrasting means thinking about similarities and differences. Two or more concepts are grouped together because of shared features, but they are distinguished from one another by other features. As you read this lesson, think about ways in which Syrians and Romans differed in their treatment of Jewish rebellions.

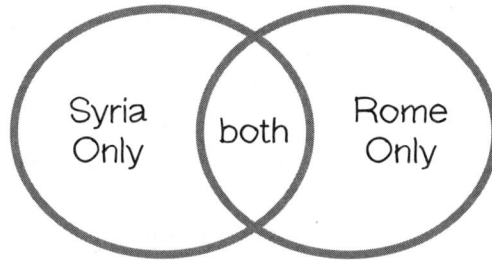

Syria Only   both   Rome Only

READING STRATEGY: QUESTIONS

1. Who tried to impose Greek culture and beliefs on the Jews?

   _____

   _____

2. Who forced the Jews to move out of Judea?

   _____

   _____

3. Who used force to put down Jewish rebellions?

   _____

   _____

CHAPTER 10

CHAPTER 10 | REVIEW The Hebrew Kingdoms

Reading Skill and Strategy

Reading Skill: Understanding Cause and Effect

Causes are the events, conditions, and other reasons that lead to an event. Causes happen before the event in time; they explain why it happened. Effects are the results or consequences of the event. As you look back over the following chapter, think about the causes and effects of various events.

READING STRATEGY: QUESTIONS

1. What were some effects of the Hebrew belief in one God?

_____

_____

_____

2. What was one effect of the Exodus from Egypt?

_____

_____

_____

3. What was one effect of the Jewish struggle against Roman authority?

_____

_____

_____

The Hebrew Kingdoms

Belief Systems
- The Hebrews worshiped one God.
- The beliefs of the Hebrews helped them survive difficult times.
- After being expelled from their homeland, most Jews remained loyal to their beliefs.

Geography
- Abraham left Mesopotamia to settle in Canaan.
- Hebrew slaves left Egypt and returned to Canaan.
- Hebrew captives left Babylon and returned to the kingdom of Judah.

Government
- The Hebrews built a small but influential nation, Israel, that later divided into the kingdoms of Israel and Judah.
- The Jews fought against foreign control by the Assyrians, Babylonians, and Romans.
- Jewish resistance to Roman rule hastened their departure from their homeland.

CHAPTER 11 | LESSON 1 The Geography of Greece

Reading Skill and Strategy

Reading Skill: Understanding Effect

An effect is an event or action that is the result of a cause. Historians study effects to understand the long-term impact of events and actions. Learning this skill will help you to see how events across time are connected. Fill in the chart below by listing the effect of each cause listed.

Causes	Effects
Mountains cover most of Greece.	
Several seas surround Greece.	
Greece traded with other regions.	

READING STRATEGY: QUESTIONS

Select the letter of the cause that led to each effect.

Effects

_____ **1.** failure to unite under one government

_____ **2.** outdoor activities a big part of culture

_____ **3.** a shortage of good farmland

_____ **4.** fish being a major part of diet

_____ **5.** adopting the alphabet

_____ **6.** learning to use coins

Causes

a. a mild climate

b. rugged mountains hindering travel

c. trade with the Phoenicians

d. rocky soil

e. doing business with other trading peoples

f. living close to the sea

CHAPTER 11

CHAPTER 11 | LESSON 2 Beliefs and Customs

Reading Skill and Strategy

Reading Skill: Making Generalizations

A generalization is a broad judgment that you make based on specific pieces of information. This skill is useful for seeing patterns in history. On the chart below, record specific information about the religious beliefs and literature of ancient Greece.

Greek Religious Beliefs	Greek Literature

READING STRATEGY: QUESTIONS

1. Consider the story of Prometheus. Judging from that story, what generalizations can you make about the Greek gods?

   _____

   _____

   _____

2. Consider the role that the gods played in the *Odyssey*. How did the Greeks seem to view the character of their gods? Explain.

   _____

   _____

   _____

CHAPTER 11

CHAPTER 11 ⏐ LESSON 3 The City-State and Democracy

Reading Skill and Strategy

Reading Skill: Categorizing

When you categorize, you sort information into useful groups. This skill will help you to organize study material and to prepare outlines for papers. Categorize the information about government in Greece, found in Lesson 3, by recording it on the chart below.

Types of Government		
Monarchy	Oligarchy	Democracy

READING STRATEGY: QUESTIONS

1. Which of the three types of government listed on your chart was most similar to aristocracy? Explain.

   _____

   _____

   _____

2. Which city-state was most closely linked to the category of democracy? Explain.

   _____

   _____

   _____

CHAPTER 11

CHAPTER 11 | LESSON 4 Sparta and Athens

Reading Skill and Strategy

Reading Skill: Comparing and Contrasting

You can use this skill to find the ways that things are similar and different. You might apply it to people, cultures, governments, artistic styles, or events. In this way, you will start to see patterns in history. Use the Venn diagram below to compare and contrast Athens and Sparta.

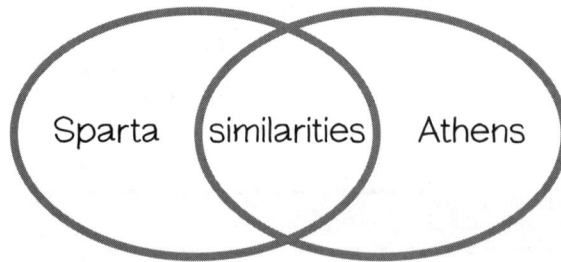

Sparta (similarities) Athens

READING STRATEGY: QUESTIONS

1. How were the lives of Athenian and Spartan citizens similar and different?

   _____

   _____

   _____

2. How was education in Sparta similar to or different from education in Athens?

   _____

   _____

   _____

CHAPTER 11

CHAPTER 11 | REVIEW Ancient Greece

Reading Skill and Strategy

Reading Skill: Making Inferences

The skill of making inferences helps you to understand the importance of what you read. To make an inference, use your own knowledge to come up with ideas about the text. Study the chart below and then answer the questions beneath it by making inferences.

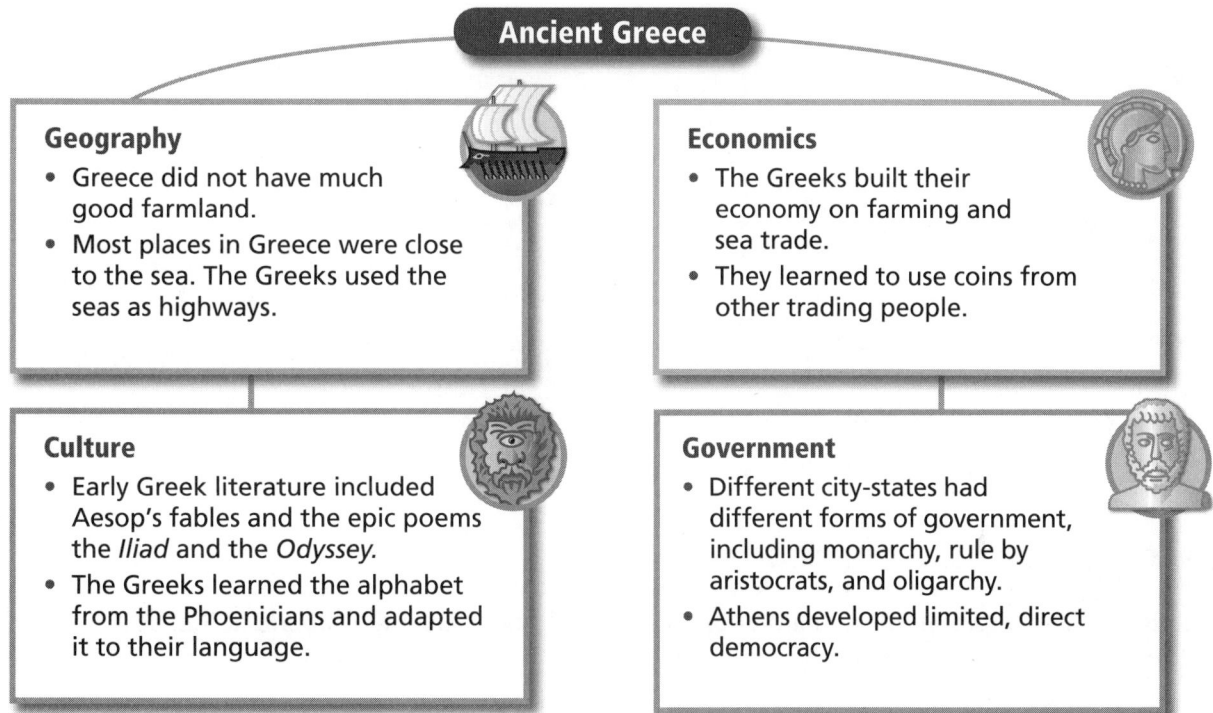

Ancient Greece

Geography
- Greece did not have much good farmland.
- Most places in Greece were close to the sea. The Greeks used the seas as highways.

Economics
- The Greeks built their economy on farming and sea trade.
- They learned to use coins from other trading people.

Culture
- Early Greek literature included Aesop's fables and the epic poems the *Iliad* and the *Odyssey*.
- The Greeks learned the alphabet from the Phoenicians and adapted it to their language.

Government
- Different city-states had different forms of government, including monarchy, rule by aristocrats, and oligarchy.
- Athens developed limited, direct democracy.

READING STRATEGY: QUESTIONS

1. Why did so many forms of government develop in ancient Greece?

   _____

   _____

   _____

2. Why would a system of writing such as the alphabet be an important skill for a trading people to have?

   _____

   _____

   _____

CHAPTER 11

CHAPTER 12 | LESSON 1 The Golden Age of Greece

Reading Skill and Strategy

Reading Skill: Finding Main Ideas

A main idea is a statement that summarizes the most important point a paragraph, section, or lesson makes. Sometimes the main idea is clearly stated in a first or last sentence. At other times, you must use the details in the reading as clues to the main idea. Use the graphic below to identify three goals of Pericles, a leader of Athens. Write your answer in a summary sentence.

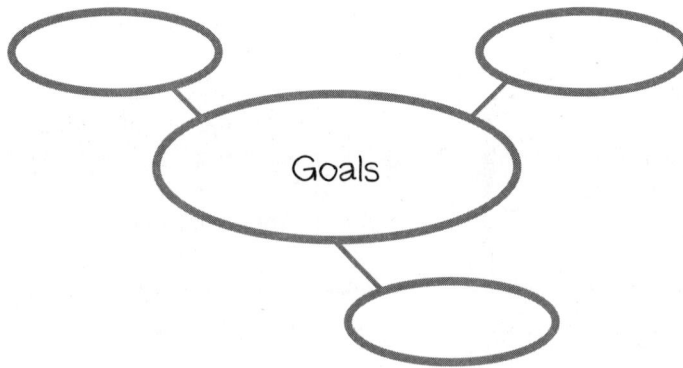

READING STRATEGY: QUESTIONS

1. Read the paragraph titled, "Paid Public Officials." Then select the statement that best expresses the main idea of the paragraph.

   ____ Most public officials were unpaid when Pericles became leader of Athens.

   ____ Only free males over 18 with Athenian parents were considered citizens in Athens.

   ____ To spread power more evenly, Pericles changed the rules for holding public office.

2. Read the paragraph titled, "Athens Dominates the Delian League." Then select the statement that best expresses the main idea of the paragraph.

   ____ Athens expanded its power over the Greek city-states and became an empire.

   ____ The fleet of Athens was the strongest in the Mediterranean region.

   ____ The transfer of the Delian League's treasury to Athens helped strengthen Athens power.

CHAPTER 12 LESSON 2 Peloponnesian War

Reading Skill and Strategy

Reading Skill: Comparing and Contrasting

Comparing things means looking for similarities. Contrasting things means looking for differences. Looking for similarities and differences between two or more things may help you understand events, ideas, beliefs, or people. Fill in the chart below to help you understand the difference in the way Sparta and Athens waged war against each other.

War Strategy	
Athens	Sparta

READING STRATEGY: QUESTIONS

1. Read the paragraph titled, "Athens Disliked." Select one of the questions you might ask that would help you contrast Athens and Sparta.

   ___ Why did other city-states dislike Athens?

   ___ What was the purpose of the league led by Sparta?

   ___ Why did Pericles punish city-states that resisted Athens?

2. Read the section titled, "The War Rages." Select one of the questions you might ask that would help you contrast Athens and Sparta.

   ___ What were the strengths of the two city-states?

   ___ What does the term *plague* mean?

   ___ Where was the Peloponnesian War fought?

CHAPTER 12

CHAPTER 12 | LESSON 3 Alexander the Great

Reading Skill and Strategy

Reading Skill: Understanding Cause and Effect

A cause may be a person, an event, or an idea that makes something happen. An effect is something that results from a cause. There are many examples of cause and effect in the study of history. In the chart below causes that allowed Alexander to rise to power are listed. Fill in the effects side of the chart.

Causes	Effects
Weak governments	
New weapons of warfare	
Foreign conquests	

READING STRATEGY: QUESTIONS

1. Read the section, "Alexander Defeats Persia." Pick the statement that best describes the cause of Persia's defeat by Alexander.

   ____ The Egyptians crowned Alexander pharaoh.

   ____ Alexander destroyed the city-state of Troy.

   ____ Alexander successfully used bold military tactics.

2. Read the section, "Alexander's Other Conquests." Pick the statement that best describes the effect of Alexander's death at the age of 32.

   ____ No single person could control the entire empire so it broke up.

   ____ One of Alexander's generals was voted the official leader.

   ____ The Persians reclaimed their empire and defeated Alexander's troops.

CHAPTER 12 | LESSON 4 The Legacy of Greece

Reading Skill and Strategy

Reading Skill: Finding Main Ideas

A main idea is a statement that summarizes the most important point made in a paragraph, section, or lesson. Sometimes the main idea is clearly stated in a first or last sentence. At other times, you must use the details in the reading as clues to the main idea. Use the chart below to list the main ideas in the categories listed.

The Arts & Architecture	History & Philosophy	Science & Technology

READING STRATEGY: QUESTIONS

1. Before you read the section, "History, Philosophy, and Democracy," look at the headings. Then, on the lines below, write a question about the main idea of the section. When you have finished reading the section review the question and write the answer.

   _____

   _____

   _____

   _____

2. Look at the diagram labeled, "Greek Astronomy" at the bottom of page 416. Then, on the lines below, write a statement summarizing the main idea of the diagram.

   _____

   _____

   _____

Reading Skill and Strategy

Reading Skill: Making Inferences

When you infer you interpret information by looking at what is stated and using your common sense and previous knowledge. You may ask yourself what a set of ideas or facts mean. Look at the Visual Summary on Classical Greece below. What can you infer about Greek Science and Technology?

READING STRATEGY: QUESTIONS

1. Study the section on Government in the Visual Summary on Classical Greece. Pick a statement that best shows an inference from that information, your common sense, and previous knowledge.

___ Alexander's empire was larger than the United States.

___ The form of government in the United States has its roots in Greece.

___ Greek direct democracy is a result of Alexander's conquests.

2. Study the section on Culture in the Visual Summary on Classical Greece. Pick a statement that best shows an inference from that information, your common sense, and previous knowledge.

___ There was no history before the Greeks started writing it down.

___ The Greeks used logic to help write history and drama.

___ Western philosophy may be grounded in different ideas than Eastern philosophy.

Classical Greece

Culture
- Developed the basis of western philosophy
- Established rules for the writing of history
- Set out rules of logic

Arts
- Created drama
- Used the ideal as the basis for the arts
- Set artistic standards for art and architecture

Science & Technology
- Made important discoveries about Earth and the planets
- Devised new mathematics
- Developed inventions such as compound pulley and water lifting devices

Government
- Created and used direct democracy
- Expanded citizen participation in government
- Alexander built an enormous empire including land in Asia, Africa, and Europe

CHAPTER 12

CHAPTER 13 | LESSON 1 The Geography of Ancient Rome

Reading Skill and Strategy

Reading Skill: Categorizing

Categorizing helps you organize similar kinds of information into groups. As you read the lesson, record what you learn about ancient Rome in the diagram below. Write down details about Rome's early history in the "Beginnings" box. List details about Rome's location in the "Geography" box. And give details about the early Roman people in the "Early Romans" box.

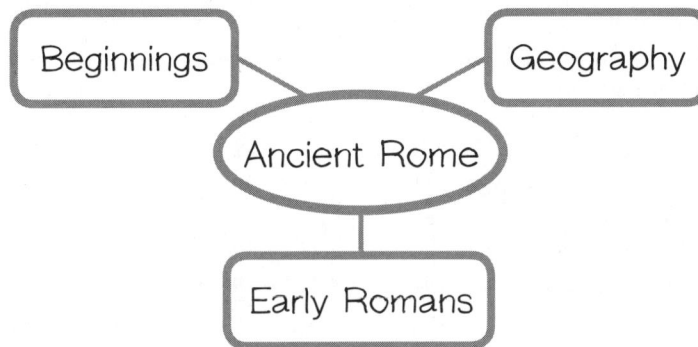

```
    Beginnings              Geography

            Ancient Rome

            Early Romans
```

READING STRATEGY: QUESTIONS

1. Which of the following details would you categorize under the heading "Geography"? Place a checkmark beside the correct detail.

   _____ The Tiber River helped protect ancient Rome from invaders.

   _____ According to legend, Romulus traced Rome's boundaries around the Palatine Hill.

   _____ Most early Romans lived on farms.

2. Which of the following sections provides details that can be categorized under the heading "Beginnings"? Place a checkmark beside the correct section.

   _____ Italian Peninsula

   _____ Farm Life

   _____ The Founding of Rome

3. Under which category would you place each of the following? Write "Beginnings," "Geography," or "Early Romans" beside each statement.

   _____ Two mountain ranges helped protect Rome.

   _____ Many Roman farmers lived in extended families.

   _____ Italy' location on the Mediterranean made it easier for Rome to conquer new territories.

CHAPTER 13 | LESSON 2 The Roman Republic

Reading Skill and Strategy

Reading Skill: Understanding Cause and Effect

A cause is an event. An effect is the result or consequence of the event. One event often has more than one result. Historians examine cause-and-effect relationships to understand how events are related and why they took place. Use the following questions to help you identify the effects of the causes listed in the diagram below.

Causes	Effects
Romans no longer wanted a monarchy.	
Plebeians were not equal to the patricians.	
Rome expanded its territories.	

READING STRATEGY: QUESTIONS

1. What was the result when the Romans no longer wanted a monarchy? Place a check beside the correct answer and record it in the diagram above.

   _____ Cincinnatus was made dictator.

   _____ They founded a republic.

   _____ Rome fought the Punic Wars.

2. What were two consequences of the inequality between patricians and plebeians? Place a check beside the two correct answers and record them in the diagram above.

   _____ Two classes arose as Rome developed into a complex civilization.

   _____ The inequality caused tension between the two classes.

   _____ The patricians passed the Twelve Tables, which established basic rights for Roman citizens.

3. What happened when Rome expanded its territories? Place a check beside two results and record them in the diagram above.

   _____ Rich Roman farmers became richer.

   _____ Rome captured and destroyed Carthage.

   _____ The gap between rich and poor in Roman society grew wider.

CHAPTER 13 | LESSON 3 Rome Becomes an Empire

Reading Skill and Strategy

Reading Skill: Constructing Time Lines

When you place events in order on a time line, you get a sense of the relationships among events. As you read the lesson, put events that happened in Rome between 100 B.C. and A.D. 14. Remember that dates in the B.C. era should follow in descending order; that is, from greater to smaller numbers. Dates in the A.D. era should follow in ascending order; that is, from smaller to greater numbers.

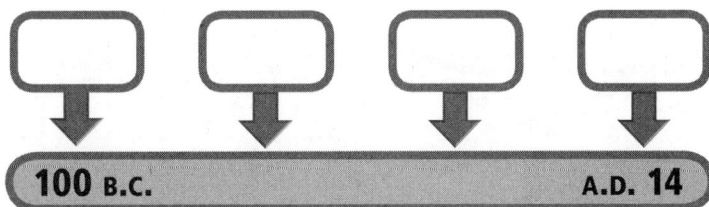

READING STRATEGY: QUESTIONS

1. What is the correct order of the following dates? Number the dates from 1 to 4.

   _____ A.D. 14

   _____ 44 B.C.

   _____ 27 B.C.

   _____ 100 B.C.

2. What is the correct order of the following events? Number the events from 1 to 4.

   _____ Caesar was named dictator for life.

   _____ Augustus became ruler of Rome.

   _____ Caesar was assassinated.

   _____ Caesar was appointed the sole Roman ruler.

CHAPTER 13 | LESSON 4 The Daily Life of Romans

Reading Skill and Strategy

Reading Skill: Summarizing

When you summarize a passage, you identify only its main ideas and important details. In the diagram below, write the title of each of the lesson's three sections and the section's main idea. In the numbered items, list the section's most important details. Feel free to list more than two details. Use the questions below to help you identify and record the main idea and supporting details. Then write a summary of the lesson.

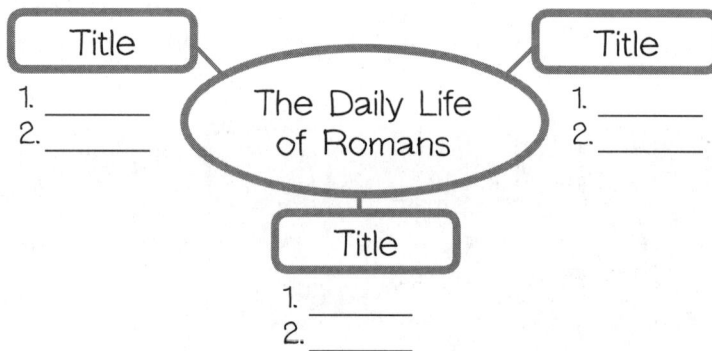

```
        Title                              Title
    1. _____        The Daily Life     1. _____
    2. _____         of Romans         2. _____

                        Title
                    1. _____
                    2. _____
```

READING STRATEGY: QUESTIONS

1. Match each main idea statement below with the appropriate section. On each line, write "Family and Society," "Roman Beliefs," or "Life in Roman Cities."

    _____ Roman cities had many problems, but they were also places of interesting innovations and entertainments.

    _____ The Romans worshiped many gods, and their religious beliefs were linked with government.

    _____ Roman men, women, and children had definite roles in family life and in society.

2. Match the details below with the appropriate section. On each line, write "Family and Society," "Roman Beliefs," or "Life in Roman Cities."

    _____ The Roman government provided practical solutions for city problems as well as entertainment.

    _____ The Romans borrowed many of their gods from the Greeks.

    _____ The large numbers of people in Roman cities resulted in overcrowding, dirt, noise, and unemployment.

    _____ Roman gods were also symbols of the state.

    _____ Slaves made up the largest—and lowest—class in Roman society.

CHAPTER 13 | REVIEW The Rise of Rome

Reading Skill and Strategy

Reading Skill: Understanding Cause and Effect

As you have learned, cause-and-effect relationships help you understand how events are related and why they took place. Use the information in the visual summary to the right to identify cause-and-effect relationships in ancient Rome.

READING STRATEGY: QUESTIONS

1. What happened as a result of Rome's location? Place a checkmark beside the correct answer.

____ A vigorous trade developed in the Roman Empire.

____ Romans worshiped many gods.

____ Rome was protected from its enemies and was able to reach and conquer other lands.

2. How did the Roman government respond to the problems of city life? Place a checkmark beside the correct answer.

____ Government was linked with religion.

____ The government built aqueducts and sanitation systems.

____ Roman government influenced modern republics.

The Rise of Rome

Geography
- Hills and the Tiber River helped protect Rome from enemies.
- Rome's location in Italy made it easier to reach and conquer other lands.

Culture
- Roman family life and society were highly structured.
- Romans built aqueducts and sanitation systems to ease the problems of city life.

Government
- The Roman Republic had a government divided into three parts.
- Roman government influenced modern republics.

Economics
- A vigorous trade developed in the Roman Empire.
- A common currency united the empire.

Belief Systems
- Romans worshiped many gods.
- Roman religion was linked with government.

CHAPTER 14 | LESSON 1 The Origins of Christianity

Reading Skill and Strategy

Reading Skill: Explaining Sequence

Sequencing events means putting things in the order in which they happened. Historians need to figure out the order in which things happened to get an accurate sense of the relationships among events. As you read this lesson, figure out the sequence, or time order, of important events in the early years of Christianity.

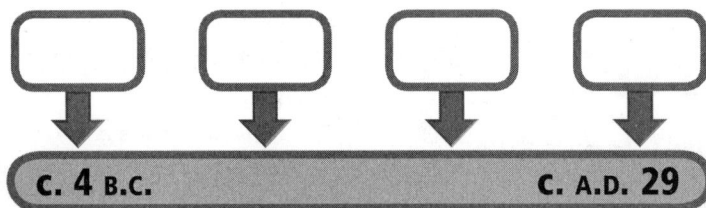

C. 4 B.C.   C. A.D. 29

READING STRATEGY: QUESTIONS

> • Jesus dies in Jerusalem.
> • Jesus is arrested and put on trial.
> • Jesus is born in Bethlehem.
> • Jesus gathers his disciples.

1. Which of the above events happened first?

_____

_____

2. Which of the above events happened last?

_____

_____

CHAPTER 14 | LESSON 2 The Early Christians

Reading Skill and Strategy

Reading Skill: Finding Main Ideas

Finding the main idea–the most important point–of a passage will increase your understanding of the material. This lesson discusses the changes in the early Christian Church. Record details about this main idea in a web diagram.

Changes in the Early Christian Church

READING STRATEGY: QUESTIONS

1. How was early Christianity unlike other religions of the time?

_____

_____

_____

2. Why has Paul's influence on Christianity remained strong?

_____

_____

_____

CHAPTER 14 | LESSON 3 Rome and Christianity

Reading Skill and Strategy

Reading Skill: Finding Main Ideas

The main idea is a statement that sums up the most important point of a paragraph, a pssage, an article, or a lesson. Determining the main idea will increase your understanding as you read about historic events, people, and places. Main ideas are supported by details and examples. In Lesson 3, look at the main heads in the lesson: Rome's Policy Toward Other Religions, The Conversion of Constantine, and Beginnings of the Roman Catholic Church. Try to pick out a couple of main ideas under each head.

Rome's Attitude Toward Christianity

READING STRATEGY: QUESTIONS

1. What was Rome's policy toward other religions?

   _____

   _____

2. Why was Constantine's conversion important?

   _____

   _____

3. On what were early Christian religious rites called sacraments based?

   _____

   _____

CHAPTER 14 | REVIEW The Birth of Christianity

Reading Skill and Strategy

Reading Skill: Finding Main Ideas

The main idea is a statement that sums up the most important point of a paragraph, a passage, an article, or a lesson. Determining the main idea will increase your understanding as you read about historic events, people, and places. Main ideas are supported by details and examples.

READING STRATEGY: QUESTIONS

1. Upon the beliefs of what other religion did Christianity build?

_____

_____

_____

2. Where did Paul make his missionary journeys?

_____

_____

_____

3. Why was Rome threatened by Christianity?

_____

_____

_____

The Birth of Christianity

Belief Systems
- Christianity built upon Jewish beliefs.
- The disciples of Jesus believed that he was the Messiah.
- Christians believe that Jesus rose from the dead and that this made an afterlife possible.
- Jesus' disciples and, later, other apostles like Paul spread the teachings of Jesus.

Geography
- Paul traveled around the eastern Roman Empire trying to convince Gentiles to believe in Jesus.

Government
- Jews and Christians challenged the authority of Rome.
- Constantine converted to Christianity and made it one of the official religions of the empire.
- The Christian church developed into a complex institution.

CHAPTER 15 | LESSON 1 An Empire in Decline

Reading Skill and Strategy

Reading Skill: Understanding Cause and Effect

A cause may be a person, an event, or an idea that makes something happen. An effect is something that results from a cause. There are many examples of cause and effect in the study of history. In the chart below, causes of the decline of the Roman Empire are listed. Fill in some effects for each cause.

Causes	Effects
Food shortages, wars, and political conflicts occur.	
Diocletian splits the empire.	
Constantine unites the empire.	

READING STRATEGY: QUESTIONS

1. Read the section "Weakness in the Empire." Select the statement that best describes the cause of a weakened Roman defense on the empire's borders.

   _____ Romans had little money and weak troops to defend the empire.

   _____ Barbarian forces continually attacked the capital city of Rome.

   _____ There was no food along the border so invaders moved into the empire.

2. Read the section "Constantine Continues Reform." Select the statement that best describes the effect of the death of Constantine.

   _____ The empire was reunited under Diocletian.

   _____ The empire's capital was moved to Byzantium.

   _____ The empire was permanently divided into two parts.

CHAPTER 15

CHAPTER 15 | LESSON 2 The Fall of the Roman Empire

Reading Skill and Strategy

Reading Skill: Explaining Sequence

Sequence is the order in which a set of events happen. When you follow a set of events through a time period you may be able to develop an understanding of how the events are related and what that may mean. In the graphic below fill in events that help bring an end to the Roman Empire.

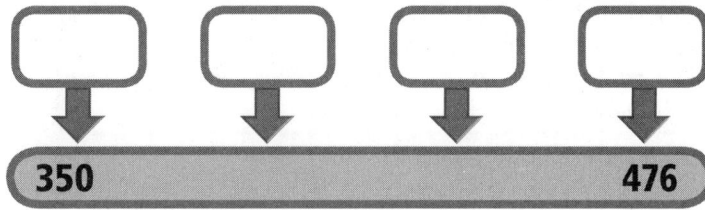

350   **476**

READING STRATEGY: QUESTIONS

1. After reading Lesson 2, pick the correct answer to the question, "Which invasion occurred last?"

____The Goths

____ The Byzantines

____ The Huns

2. After reading Lesson 2, pick the statement that shows how the events on the time line above are related.

____ These events show that the Roman Empire weakened and fell apart.

____ These events show that it was only the barbarian invasions that caused Rome's fall.

____ These events show that Attila the Hun was responsible for the fall of Rome.

CHAPTER 15

CHAPTER 15 | LESSON 3 The Byzantine Empire

Reading Skill and Strategy

Reading Skill: Summarizing

When you summarize you restate the main idea in your own words. You may wish to include some important details supporting the main idea. Use the headings to help you look for the main ideas. In the box below write a summary sentence for each of the three topics about the Byzantine Empire.

Byzantine Empire	
Justinian	
Split in Christian church	
Role of church in government	

READING STRATEGY: QUESTIONS

1. Read the section "Preserving Roman Culture." Then write a summary sentence about information in the section.

   _____

   _____

2. Read the section "The Church Divides." Then write a summary sentence about information in the section.

   _____

   _____

CHAPTER 15

CHAPTER 15 | LESSON 4 The Legacy of Rome

Reading Skill and Strategy

Reading Skill: Finding Main Ideas

A main idea is a statement that summarizes the most important point made in a paragraph, section, or lesson. Sometimes the main idea is clearly stated in a first or last sentence. At other times, you must use the details in the reading as clues to the main idea. Use the graphic below to list the main ideas about Roman legacies.

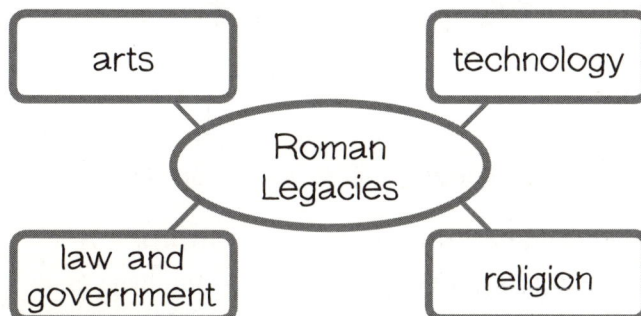

READING STRATEGY: QUESTIONS

1. Read the paragraph "Aqueducts." Select the sentence from the paragraph that presents the main idea and copy it on the lines below.

   _____

   _____

2. Read the section "Roads." Select the sentence that presents the main idea of the section.

   _____ The Roman highway system served a dual purpose—defense and trade.

   _____ Roman road builders were famous for their quality roads.

   _____ The Roman road system increased trade throughout the empire.

CHAPTER 15

CHAPTER 15 | REVIEW Rome's Decline and Legacy

Reading Skill and Strategy

Reading Skill: Comparing and Contrasting

Comparing things means looking for similarities. Contrasting things means looking for differences. Looking for similarities and differences between two or more things may help you understand events, ideas, beliefs, or people. Study the Visual Summary of Chapter 15 What elements of the Roman Empire do both the eastern and western empire share?

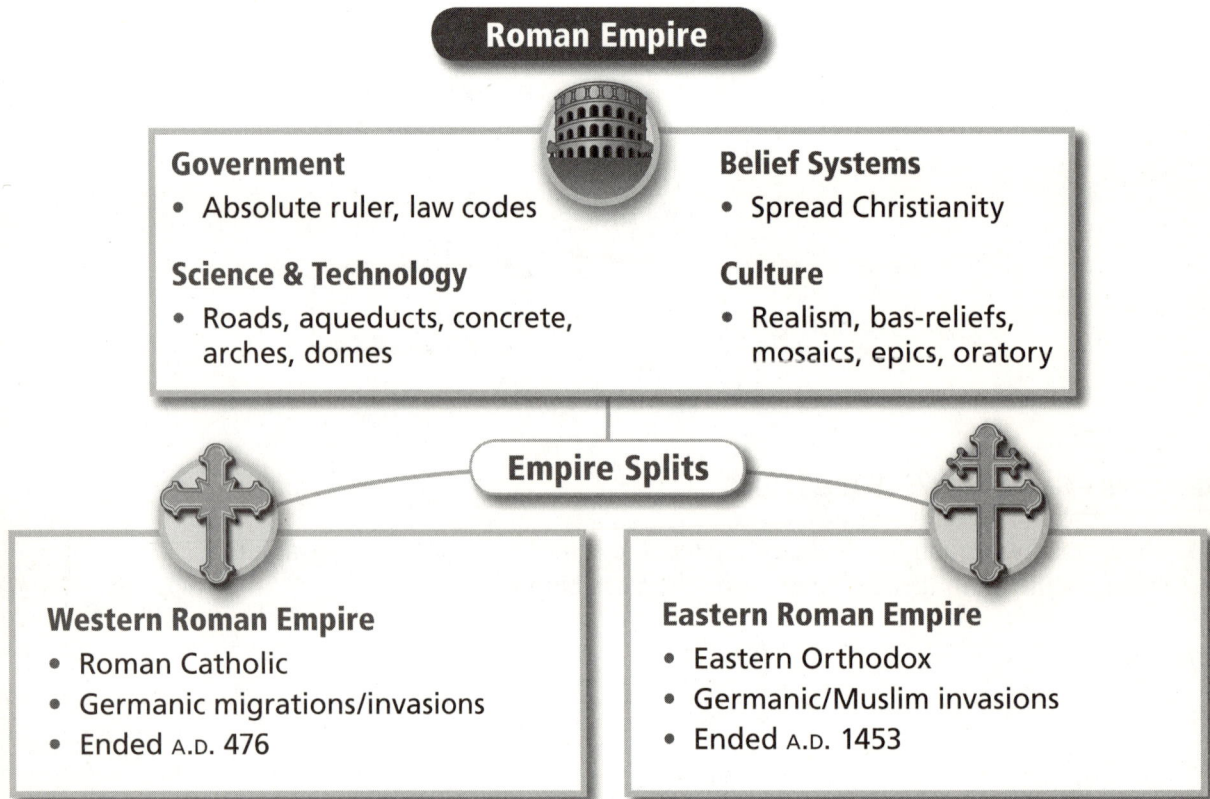

Roman Empire

Government
- Absolute ruler, law codes

Belief Systems
- Spread Christianity

Science & Technology
- Roads, aqueducts, concrete, arches, domes

Culture
- Realism, bas-reliefs, mosaics, epics, oratory

Empire Splits

Western Roman Empire
- Roman Catholic
- Germanic migrations/invasions
- Ended A.D. 476

Eastern Roman Empire
- Eastern Orthodox
- Germanic/Muslim invasions
- Ended A.D. 1453

READING STRATEGY: QUESTIONS

1. Study the Visual Summary. Which of the following statements is true?

   _____ Only the Western Roman Empire suffered German invasions.

   _____ Only the Eastern Roman Empire remained Christian.

   _____ Only the Eastern Roman Empire lasted until the 1400s.

2. Study the Visual Summary. Which of the following statements is true?

   _____ Both the Eastern and Western empires broke up before 1000 AD.

   _____ Both the Eastern and Western empires had a tradition of law codes.

   _____ Both the Eastern and Western empires practiced Roman Catholicism.